BOUT THAT LIFE

LEADERSHIP LESSONS FOR THE URBAN PROFESSIONAL

by Rahshib Thomas

RahshibThomas.com Publishing

in association with Omniversal Publishing

Omniversal Publishing House

5510 Greenwich Drive

Arlington, Texas 76018

Omniversal Publishing House is a subsidiary of

Moksha-Media.com

The Holy Bible, King James Version, in the public domain.

All quotes from A Course in Miracles are from the public domain, 1975. Foudation for Inner Peace. P.O. Box 598, Mill Valley, 94942- 0598, www.acim.org and info@acim.org.

Library of Congress Control Number:

2016901286

Print ISBN: 978-1-48357-868-2

e-book ISBN: 978-1-48357-869-9

Book Cover Design by Daymond E. Lavine of Moksha Media, moksha-media.com

Printed in USA by BookBaby.com

10 9 8 7 6 5 4 3 2 1

Publisher's Note

Dedication

Love

Patience

Kindness

Truth

All gifts

Made of spirit

Too lofty for the young

The only gift I knew

Was that God gave me a sister

And she was all mine

For My Family, blood and bonds, Teachers, Guides and Healers in My Life.

My mother, Dinise, my father, William McKinley (Rashid Waheed), April and David McFarland, The Neville/Joseph Family, The Thomas/Schley Family, Keithen Jones, The Legends: Stephen Evans, Warren Champ, Warren Glapion, Ahakim Lacy. Crystal Williams Eleby-El, Paul Carrick Brunson, Arva Rice, The Casa Trussell-Burgos, The Heartbeats: Tiffany Thomas, Joe Randolph, Pamela Perkins, Rita Lassiter. Marc Morial and the National Urban League, Ray Bruce, Paul D. Gustely, Jeanne Lynch, Jenny Herman and Jenny Lucas, The Groomer Keith Williams, Grant and The Hayes Family, Wiky Toussaint, Chris Cooper Live. Momentum Education: Robin Lynn, Robinson Lynn, and Sylvia High of Aiming High Inc.

TABLE OF CONTENTS

FOREWORD

Bout That Life: Leadership Lessons for the Urban Professional uniquely provides a roadmap for success from a community room to a boardroom for today's young urban professional. Rahshib Thomas has developed his personal brand while building the leadership potential of others through positions of increasing leadership at the iconic nonprofit organizations New York Urban League (NYUL) and National Urban League Young Professionals (NULYP). Rahshib has mastered talent development in roles of hospitality and real estate as well as volunteer training for Momentum Education. In **Bout That Life**, Rahshib weaves real life lessons learned from his professional and personal leadership journey with concrete advice, tips and exercises. Every page of **Bout That Life** reflects Rahshib's experience in coaching, training and encouraging other young professionals to discover their talents, hold themselves accountable, and constantly improve. This book is a must-read for any millennial interested in becoming his or her best self.

Arva Rice

CEO of the New York Urban League (NYUL)

Success is not separate from who we are.

~ Rahshib

PREFACE

Happiness is where we are. I began to wonder why, on many of the television shows I watched, so many people would say "I got burned out on Wall Street" or "I lost interest." This made me wonder how anyone could be happy in their profession and remain right where they were.

I wondered. What did I think it was? What did I think would help? I built my own toolbox and gathered leadership lessons that every urban professional could use to define and refine his or her own leadership story and journey.

I wrote this book to help others find their own authentic voices in leadership. It was my desire to educate others about the success that could be gained by translating neighborhood experiences to boardroom triumphs. My book describes effective and potent leadership tips and practices for the urban professional. It also tells my story as a young professional. This book is full of practices filled with swag and spicy attitude!

INTRODUCTION: HOW DID ALL OF THIS GET STARTED?

I once had a friend who grew up on a different side of the tracks. I initially met him when I was 17 and he was 15 years of age. Our friendship was valuable during my high school, college, and early career years because it helped me understand how differently people lived. When we hung out across the tracks, I authentically connected with the people he knew. I met those whom I had been taught to stay away from. I met others whom I thought had no drive to succeed and contribute to the community, but I learned otherwise. The relationship I had with my friend allowed me to truly value others. It allowed me to see things from my own vantage point opposed to that of my mother or the minister. Yet, my friend and I struggled through many conflicts because we were very different. He was fun to be with because he practically owned the night. Yet, I saw myself as the conservative and ambitious one. He liked to live on the edge and have run-ins with the law. Those activities were ones I was not willing to participate in.

When it was time for me to head off to college, my friend became interested in the college admission process. After I told him about it, he wound up going to the same college I went to. Coincidentally, he became my next door neighbor in a two-unit suite. We even shared a connecting bathroom. However, his time at college with me did not last very long. He was expelled for smoking weed in his suite and quickly thereafter had to exit the premises.

Fast forward a few years later, I graduated from college on a Saturday afternoon and got a job the following Tuesday morning at a historic hotel. I took the job just because it was work... not because it was an employment position related to my college major. It was a whirlwind as I embarked on my career immediately after college, and I was glad that I had not tried smoking weed that I was offered just before my graduation by a football player. I would have been sure to fail the pre-employment drug screening.

After eleven months of working at the front desk of the hotel, I applied for a human resources recruiter position. I got the job. With that opportunity came a tap on my shoulder to participate in a community organization on a volunteer basis. At that time, the Clinton Administration was implementing the Welfare Reform Program. Many people were in welfare-to-work job trainings. I got to know a job trainer named Mona working for the historic civil rights organization, the Urban League of Greater New Orleans (ULGNO). One day, she came to my office and asked me to interview candidates for her. She informed me that if I liked them, I could hire them, but if I did not, I had to provide feedback so they could improve the training. This Urban League trainer also presented me with a membership application to the ULGNO. I did not know it then, but that was the beginning my life journey through leadership development and community service.

As the next chapter of my life began, my friend from across the tracks and I reconnected through a mutual friend of ours. Before I knew it, I was back in the streets of New Orleans partying hard. I also had my own car. With my new car and my new career, I thought I had made it! Meanwhile, because of my volunteerism with the Urban League, I began to get invited to many functions throughout the city of New Orleans. Thanks to connections made through my job, I was asked to participate in and plan forums, workshops and fundraisers...all things I had no idea how to do. However, I tried my very best because I was honored to be a part of it all. I began to be surrounded by people I saw on the news or heard stories about regarding their high-profile families. They were people whom I had previously admired from afar. Our degrees of separation lessened, and I began to sit at the table with them, although I often did not converse with them. I was awkward at that time. Additionally, I was battling with my self-esteem and issues surrounding my sexuality. Basically, I was a mess. But fortunately, I was raised well enough to know to "keep on keeping on," as my mother would sometimes say. I knew that work had to get done, and I had to do it.

I loved life, and I wanted to be in the streets of New Orleans. Like many other young professionals starting their careers, I struggled to acclimate to office life, time budgeting and self-management. I also did not understand the way to manage expectations upward through the leadership chain. However, I was dedicated and serious about the work I was doing. As part of my work activities, I often traveled to various events and job fairs. I loved doing that. After long work days, I chose to go without my friend. Eventually, arguments between us ensued. When I shared with him where I had gone or whom I had met, he pointed out to me that I never invited him.

I did not have the 'Rahshib-ism' then, but I knew enough to manage my brand. As my mother would say "live to tell about it another day." With that saying stuck in the back of mind, I began to take life more seriously. I still occasionally went to dive bars and ran the streets with my friend. However, I split my time between those activities and also going to social events and gatherings for my job. I preferred the social gatherings more because they allowed me to expand my knowledge and my network. I was very ambitious then, but not yet as confident as I am today. At that time, my lack of confidence prevented me from adequately expressing my ambition to my friend.

What became blatantly obvious to me is the fact that my friend often ridiculed public figures or well-known politicians, some of the very same ones I met. He said things like "I'll see them in the French Quarter later tonight looking for something naughty." He also attempted to diminish their contribution to the community because he looked past their positive attributes to focus on vices about them he knew or assumed. However, he had quite an interesting life himself: my friend became a drag queen! I had no desire to join him in doing that; but, I soon started enjoying seeing him and other drag queens perform musical selections and pour their passion into preparing for the stage.

While my friend was fully indulging in his new life, I struggled somewhat with immersing myself in the business of corporate America. At one point, I vented to him on a daily basis about difficult situations I was facing at my job. He would say, "Why don't you quit?" And my response to him would be, "Oh no, I like the job."

The fact remains that although I struggled to adjust to my early career, I was very fortunate to work at my first company for four years. I remember having an argument with my friend after venting to him again about the ups and downs of my job while his typical response was, "Quit!" In an unsuccessful attempt to offer my very first coaching session to someone...I replied, "You were kicked out of school and fired from six jobs consecutively, so why would I take advice from you?" He called me cruel for responding to him that way. However, my response was based on a statement my mother would often say, "When people tell you how to live your life, look at how they are living theirs." Eventually, we had one too many disagreements, and the straw that broke the camel's back was when he wanted to be roommates in what would be my first apartment. I did not trust him with money, and I did not approve of his house guests. So, we parted ways. From that point forward, I focused on me and bettering the rest of my life.

Today, I am a human resource executive, leadership minister, and author of Bout That Life: Leadership Lessons for the Urban Professional. This story and others like it helped shape who I am and what I have to share with you in this book.

CHAPTER ONE
BULLET PROOF SOUL

Born in Los Angeles, I spent my formative years in Tacoma, Washington. By the time I was a teenager, my single mother, my younger sister and I had driven across the United States three times. We eventually settled in New Orleans, Louisiana. I was 16 years old, sitting on my bed in Marrero...and I knew. I just knew that I was different, and it would forever be my shame and my secret to keep. I knew that I was an abomination. Hell was certain for me. At the same time, I knew that I would have partially devoted "hook-ups." They too would be my secrets, and we would never express or explore our relationships publicly. I knew. I knew that I was given a burden to bear. Ready to burst with my eyes full of tears, I accepted what I knew. Still, I choked as I attempted to say to myself, "I'm gay." That was the moment I began to live in denial, shame and guilt.

The hook-ups came along, and just as I had predicted, we only spoke to each other in secret. When I began to attend college, exhilarating escapades took place, but they never resulted in relationships. In the back of my mind, I developed the notion that love or romantic relationships would never be possible for me. In college, as is the case with most of us, I gained a much keener understanding of the world around me. However, I learned, for the first time, that sexual harassment was real. From time to time, I would have abusive interactions with guys. Some days, a guy might want to know all about me and question me about who I am, what I do, and if I thought he was interesting. But on other days, he might completely ignore me or even go as far as calling me names and ridiculing me in public! And of course, the usual conversations from others would ensue. "Why are you friends with Rahshib," someone might question any person I knew. "Don't you know he's gay?" Time after time, I met people, befriended them, hung out with them, and then later, for apparently no reason at all, they disconnected from me. I never heard from them again. There would be no more phone calls. There would be no more lunches together at the WigWam cafeteria...all because others would begin questioning them!

One day, I met yet another guy, and it all started out the same way. He was nice, just like all the others. He joked with me; and he complimented me too, saying, "You're smart," and "You talk proper." But this was just another way of saying, "You're not rough like the other guys." Then over the span of weeks, the joking turned into name-calling. "Smart" turned into "faggot." He yelled it across the Bayou DeSiard Bridge and out loud across the cafeteria. I put up with this disrespect because it was not the first occurrence of a guy treating me that way despite my genuine efforts to become friends with him. Again, I thought this would be my life. As I look back on this situation, I realize that I actually expected his behavior toward me. To put an end to his bullying and harassment, I walked up to him one day and directly told him that we could not be friends any-more if he chose to continue disrespecting me. He ignored my ulti-matum, and shortly thereafter, he yelled louder and more frequently at me. In the past, other guys had either completely disconnected from me in silence or with lies spread around declaring I had hit on them. However, this guy would persistently go out of his way to try to verbally attack me. I had done nothing to him to deserve that treatment. I was baffled!

Day after day, the name calling continued as I crossed Bayou DeSiard on my way to class, and I continually asked my bully to stop. Sometimes he would stop for a couple of days, then the name calling would start up again. At peculiar times, he would turn my requests for him to stop into a question of my interest in him. He would say, "You like me, don't you?" I told him I was not attracted to him, and I did not trust him. During my college years, it was common for "straight" guys to engage in sexual acts with gay guys in some hidden place. Assault would typically follow because the "straight" guy would threaten the gay guy to keep quiet about their sexual rendezvous. Again, we were not involved; yet, I needed help, and I needed it soon! Still, I was afraid to turn to anyone for assistance. To some extent, because of my feelings and my attraction toward guys, I thought I brought my situation on myself.

One day, I chose to get help, and I decided to go to the campus Community Counseling Clinic to talk to someone about what I was going through. I prepared the statements that I would say. Clearly, I would say, "Yes, I'm gay, but no I did not and never have hit on him." As I marched up the walkway to the clinic, I noticed a group of staff members heading to the same door, but from the opposite direction. One of them was a faculty member and campus liaison for an on-campus African-American fraternity. I knew his face, and he knew mine. In that moment, I panicked. I had mustered up enough courage to "come out" and seek the mental and emotional support that I needed; but, in a matter of seconds after seeing him, I retreated. I was uncomfortable, and this guy was way too close for comfort. I walked away from the building. The fraternity guy was the last of the faculty members entering the building. He looked at me. It seemed as if he wanted to speak to me; but once again, I turned away. On that day, my 20-something year-old mind was made up; emotional support was not an option for me. I was an abomination, and help was not available.

More days passed. It took additional confrontations with my bully to give me the boost of courage I needed to seek help again. This time, I went to the campus police. The officer I spoke to was a white woman, and my gaydar alerted she was a lesbian. I explained my situation to her the best way I could. I also emphasized, "Yes I'm gay, but I've done nothing to him and I've never hit on him. I just want him to leave me alone."

Later in the week while walking back to my dorm, the guy was outside near my building lobby with a group of guys and girls. There was no retreat and my only option was to walk past him. While I did so, he snarled and said, "Ain't no police gonna do me nothing. You're gonna talk to me." As I kept walking I wished and hoped the guys and girls sitting with him would've had enough common sense to ask, "Why are you bothering him?" By the end of the semester, the guy stopped bothering me, and I stopped caring. It would take me years to realize my self-worth and to learn how to prevent others from mistreating me or taking my kindness for weakness.

And Then Some...

Through this experience I know that I was supposed to learn the following:

1. *To stand up for myself.*

2. *To realize that friends don't make it difficult to be friends.*

3. *To understand that it's not enough to have a Plan A. You should have a Plan B, Plan C, and Plan D in case you have to keep trying.*

THE LAW OF FAME

Many people want what they idolize from external sources such as reality shows, coworkers, friends or constituents of various organizations. Many people compare what they have to others. They say they want it all. Sometimes they get it; yet, they often cannot withstand the rigor that it demands and the commitment it all requires. I call this the Law of Fame. Fame is a very bright light. When it shines, will you be ready to stand in its warmth and allow it to expose parts you don't typically share...the intimate you? I believe there are a few elements of fame that require one to embrace and step into. Fame is a ride to which you must get acquainted and hopefully enjoy. I've heard some say it's like riding the tail of a comet, and that it requires an abundance of giving and generosity of self. You must be "on" even when you don't feel your best. You must "inspire" even when you're weary. You must "smile" when you only want to look and observe. You must "engage" others when you just want to go somewhere and hide. We've heard many times before, fame costs; and with the next few chapters, I want to know...are you willing?

Intention Will Find You Out!
Are you in this for SERVICE or FAME?

How many times have you been willing to take a hard look at what's working or not working in your life? How many times have you engaged in pathological behavior because no one has stepped in to stop you. Are you willing to ask yourself "why?" Are you willing to explore your intentions for roots, causes and motives? This is where your ocean of concerns will boil down a river of hope. Many people obtain positions to prove a point instead of serving a cause. They want to prove to as many people as they can that they matter. They want to prove they are worthy, prove they are enough. If you start out thinking, "I want to build my resume," keep searching your heart. Poorly aligned intentions manifest when people are miserable in their roles and do not excel; yet continue to think it's about everyone else while they have forgotten to take a look at themselves.

And Then Some...

1. *Pray.*

2. *Think long term and ask, "How can I leave this better than I found it?"*

3. *Perform strength assessments and other profile assessments.*

4. *Ask others for feedback...it's a gift, even though you may not realize it.*

CHAPTER TWO
I LOST

It was an epic Saturday in the summer of 2013. The National Urban League Conference was taking place in Philadelphia, and you would swear it was the NBA Finals, the Super Bowl, American Idol Finale, a House of Cards Watch Party, and the Miss America Pageant all rolled into one event! The second vote was up after a five hour parliamentary debate. Soon after, all the votes came back, and there were 27 for the incumbent and 24 for me. My bid for National Urban League Young Professionals president came to a fiery end. I lost! It was over, and it seemed that I had nothing to show for it. Initially, this loss represented the disapproval of the work I had done and given my all with every fiber of my being since I was 23 years old. Up to the final vote, I knew that my incumbent was willing to play a game I was not. During the parliamentary debate, she retreated to her room under the stress of it all, but when it was time for the voting results to be announced, she was called back to the conference room. And poof! Just like that, my leadership role with the National Urban League Young Professionals ended. My mood disintegrated, and I simply became fatigued and hungry. As the winner took the podium, I became numb. I was in shock. I felt betrayed by a few individuals; and still, I gained a new appreciation for others. It was in that moment that I became acutely aware of who supported me and who was actually "into me" as a friend. I took note of those who were my "true" friends, not because of my title, but me...just me...no filter...no pretense...no ulterior motive. They were those who appreciated the authentic me.

A Course in Miracles Workbook Lesson 193 states, "All things are lessons God would have me learn." In my loss, one of my lessons was to realize how to be in relationships with others. At the time of the election, I was in the middle of a 90-day transformation program called "Leadership." It was a program that I became aware of during my research, training and preparation to spend two vigorous years as the president of the National Urban League Young Professionals. I soaked up any and everything I could find in an attempt to move members of my organization forward. My desire was for us to move beyond the focus on resume building and climbing the corporate ladder because I wanted to insert a little mental health awareness into routine tasks. When I searched for training guidance to give to others that dealt with the heart and the mind, I found some training for myself. That training was something that came to me at the time I needed it most!

Because of the Leadership Program (LT) that I participated in, I had a newfound personal awareness! This awareness taught me to pause in a moment of turmoil, look for options, and then choose one. I got to choose who I would become, following my defeat. After the 2013 Philadelphia Conference ended, I returned home to Harlem on a rainy Sunday. I was glad to be home. I would get to sleep in my own bed again. That night, I had dinner with the friend who introduced me to the leadership program. The first thing I articulated to him was my pain, but also how grateful I was for those who supported me. I mentioned to my friend the genuineness I felt from them in a whole new way. On Monday, however, anger showed up. It was so potent that I could hardly open my eyes. I got up, and I walked to the neighborhood coffee shop. As I walked there, I wallowed in my disappointment thinking to myself, "But I had plans for the organization!" However, as I replayed that thought in my head over and over again, the Holy Spirit spoke to me. The voice said, "You made declarations to Me, and you don't know how they're going to show up." That voice stopped me dead in my tracks. All I could think was, "Whoa! What was that?" The voice stated something contrary to those thoughts I was wallowing in. Without a doubt, after that moment, I knew my work wasn't done!

Over the course of the following weeks, my phone rang several times, but I only answered for people whom I considered to be friends. One of those callers was a mentee and president of my home National Urban League chapter. I expressed to him that I simply wanted to support the development of our membership to strengthen the organization. He asked if there was something in particular that I wanted to do with his chapter. And wow! I instantly recalled the message that I received from the Holy Spirit.

The LT had taught me to "stand in my vision and not stand my ground." Just as my close friend and mentee asked me what I wanted to do with his chapter, other chapter leaders around the country soon asked the same question, "What would you like to do?" The funny thing is this: I continued to work on behalf of the National Urban League Young Professionals, promoting it wherever I went. I began to find myself telling decisions makers things like, "I have no authority to speak on behalf of the organization, but I do think this is an organization you should do business with." Then, time and time again, decision makers would say to me, "We know who you are." It became clear to me what I now know to be true in my heart and mind as a leader, my loss at the Philadelphia Conference ushered in an awareness that leadership requires no titles. This lesson took me the longest time to learn. I also understood who my "Confidants,

Constituents, and Comrades" were as Bishop T. D. Jakes calls them in a YouTube video.

And Then Some...

Through this experience I know that I was supposed to learn the following:

1. *How to be in relationships with people.*

2. *How to access my vulnerability and create a level of intimacy with others that I was incapable of having with others before:*

   As a result of what I experienced after the campaign and election, during my own healing and awareness process, I was able to access and create a level of vulnerability and intimacy that wasn't available to me prior to the election.

3. *How to maintain relationships with people through connection, contribution and acknowledgement:*

   After a year or so after the election in Philadelphia, I reconnected with certain people, primarily, those in the Urban League whom I felt betrayed me. I was able to own who I was in the matter and recognize the part I played in any breakdown of our relationship.

4. *How to settle grievances in my life:*

   For no reason at all, "just because" as they say, I called or emailed people I had not spoken to in years. If their name popped into mind, I simply reached out to them. I then owned who I was in our relationship.

5. *How to receive support and acknowledgment from others:*

   People were typically kind to me, but I tended to equate their kindness with my volunteer efforts. Although never said (with my then scarce mindset), I used to think in the back of mind that, "Rahshib, you're only given access because of what you can do." I learned how to receive acknowledgment just for being me...nothing or no one else. With my leadership roles stripped away, I learned how to sit still long enough to receive support. To this day, I am forever grateful to be clear on that.

CHAPTER THREE
CALCULATE THE COST

*"For which of you, intending to build a tower, sitteth not down first,
and counteth the cost, whether he have sufficient to finish it?"*

~ Luke 14:28 KJV

As a volunteer on various boards, over various terms, I always heard exhausted peers say "I didn't know it was going to be this much." My knee-jerk response would be, "What did you think this was?" Many people like the idea of leadership or service opportunities, but hesitate to fully step into the rigor, accountability and urgency such roles often require.

As chapter president of the New York Urban League Young Professionals (NYULYP), I served with an executive board of dynamic, well sought-after individuals. It was the beginning of our terms, and our new New York Urban League (NYUL) CEO, Ms. Arva Rice, invited us to her home for brunch. We engaged in an ice-breaker called Bout That Life Convo Connection Activity (which is later described in the back of this book), and we ate some delicious food. My fellow board members shared with Ms. Rice their roles for NYULYP. They also shared information with her about other activities they were involved with.

A couple weeks later, Ms. Rice wanted to connect over dinner. During the dinner, she shared with me her impression of the team. She was awestruck by how busy everyone was, and she wondered if they were too busy to commit to their roles as executive board members of NYULYP. While she shared her thoughts with me, all I could think was, "What am I supposed to do? I try and try to get them to focus, but they are ambitious and working on their next big thing...I don't know where and how to support them in finding balance."

She went on to tell me something that I've been saying ever since: "Leadership must be a priority." She told me how she sets the expectation for her team to make their service a priority. It made sense to me. When she said it, I heard, "Surrender." When relaying this to other professionals and ULYP chapters, I started communicating the following way. "Your service has a beginning and end date. The request is that you make this role a priority in your life until the role ends. It's only a commitment for six months to a year, or in some instances I need you for two years."

As my leadership responsibilities increased in all areas of my life, I became acutely clear up front on time commitments and what was expected of me. This helped me to responsibly say 'yes' or 'no' to the commitments asked of me.

There is so much that can be required of you. The world often requires a huge commitment from you. Healing your family, generation, community and the planet is no joke! Once you're in it, you're in it. Leadership is a choice that must be stepped into. You can responsibly forecast or make assumptions about tangible things, but you must commit to ride the ride, stand in the light, follow when necessary and be a leader at all times. Once you choose it, it's going to happen. Don't concern yourself about when, where or how, but it is about the fact that it will happen.

And Then Some...

When you step into leadership roles, make sure that you do the following:

1. *Weigh the pros and cons. Get clear on expectations quickly.*

2. *Do the due diligence about people and situations.*

3. *Manage timelines. Build your calendar and train yourself to look ahead weekly, monthly, quarterly and yearly. Then keep going!*

4. *Ask financial questions until you get it.*

5. *Leadership vs. Membership: Members can be casual about commitments because they are observers, but Leaders are obligated to commit. Know the difference and commit.*

Success is not Separate from Who We Are

Have you ever found yourself saying "I'm not going to work hard for these people" or "this organization because it's just volunteer?" Or you say, "they don't pay me enough" and you hold back on your commitment or your true contribution? The Holy Spirit or Universe has placed you in a position to be what's wanted and needed right where you are and it requires your best: your inner best, your loving best and your generous best.

Holding back is stingy. It's also not that deep! Simply, if you're an Executive Assistant at work and volunteer on your condo board at home, your volunteerism deserves the same level of detail and attention you deliver when you are receiving a paycheck. When you think you don't know the answer, you do. When you think you don't have an idea, you do. When you think it's not the same as work, it is. Success is not separate from who you are. Be excellent all the time. Be generous with your abilities all the time. Don't withhold. You are needed. Your gifts and talents have made room for you. And know this, once you're in it, be all the way in! 100%

No man, having put his hand to the plough, and look-
ing back, is fit for the kingdom of God

~ Luke 9:62 KJV

CHAPTER FOUR
MAKE LOVE TO THE CROWD

How You Treat People Matters...

I was in my early twenties, and not only was it my first Urban League of Greater New Orleans (ULGNO) Golden Gala. I also needed a date! The obvious and available choice was my sister April. Cathy Washington, Vice President of Operations of ULGNO, had invited me to attend, and I was honored. I was also scared out of my mind. The voices in my head began to fill my thoughts with concerns about how I was going to get ready for this event. It was a black tie event, and I did not own a tuxedo at the time. I also did not know where and how to go about getting one. Let's not mention the fact that I could not afford one. I did however have a black suit, and I complemented it with a satin tie and a matching satin handkerchief and "called it a day." Basically, that combination would have to work.

The gala was at the Ernst N. Morial Convention Center. I was one of the four hundred people expected to attend. The first stop on my invitation agenda was the VIP reception. I was nervous and intimidated. My 23-year-old awkwardness was in full effect. During the reception, people passed April and I, and no one, except for Cathy, said hello. I began to feel unworthy. I also began to feel as if I didn't belong. I thought that perhaps I was trying to climb a ladder to places I was not welcome. Shame came over me, and I believed I didn't have the pedigree. Of course, no one said these things to me, but the fact that they did not say anything spoke louder to me. Little did I know, that night would be a moment in my life I would never forget.

Suddenly, a well-known public figure, the epitome of proper decorum, status and a Louisiana queen, extended her hand to me to introduce herself as if it were necessary. She said, "Hi, I'm Lindy Boggs." Wow! The U.S. Representative from 1973 to 1991 and fifth U.S. Ambassador to the Vatican said hello to lil' ol' me! I was stunned, and for a moment, I thought it was odd. No other important person even looked me in the eye. Members of the New Orleans elite were present. I had not arrived to such status, nor did my family name immediately resonate with others. However, the most important person in the room, I thought, said hello to me. She made me feel important. She saw me. It was my "Avatar" moment.

That night, Lindy Boggs was honored. Thereafter, everything became a blur to me. April took a picture with her, and I left that evening thinking I was someone to whom Lindy thought enough to say hello. Wow. The way she made me feel that night stuck with me ever since. I observed how a woman with nothing to prove to anyone floated through the room. I took note of how she worked the entire room while extending her hand with eye contact and smiling at everyone whom she encountered. Now I try to recreate, for others, that same type of moment. I've been called a social butterfly because of it. I simply want to make others know they are seen, even within in a sea of other people. As a leader, I always encourage my teams to "make love to the crowd."

"You Don't Dog Nobody"

When I was a child living on A Street in Tacoma, going outside to play was an important part of the day. On one particular day, as my sister and I were preparing for our important task of going outside, there was a knock at the door. My sister answered. It was a friend of hers. She asked April to come out and play, and April responded by saying, "I'll be outside after my mom brushes my hair." April closed the door. No more than five minutes passed, and there was another knock at the door. It was another friend of my sister. Again, that friend asked April come out and play. April declined this friend saying she didn't feel like it, even though she had just told her other friend she would join her. I recall my mother and I watching both interactions, and we both shrugged our shoulders thinking, "Did April just do that to one friend versus the other?" As soon as the door closed, and April resumed her hair brushing position at my mother's feet, my mother immediately scolded my sister for being inconsistent with her responses to her friends. She told April, "You don't dog nobody!" That phrase has stuck with me through the years, and it reminds me that I should be fair with everyone. I think about it when managing others and creating policies and procedures for organizations.

Love Thy Community

Working with the community is a true labor of love. I assumed because of the way I looked, I could go into high crime and high poverty communities and blend. Little did I realize until I moved into a transitioning neighborhood, I was part of the gentrification wave. How did I become an "outsider" and "one of them?"

It took almost four months of self-development workshops for me to realize I was being a Christian and Urban Leaguer everywhere else except on my neighborhood block. Because of my pride in purchasing an apartment in Harlem, I didn't want anyone hanging on the corner of my block, especially on my stoop. I wanted the cops to stop and frisk everyone on my block who looked suspicious. I especially wanted people checked who hung out on my block all day…those who chose to drive in and come by train only to hang out daily because it was "their block for life," yet no longer the place they physically resided. I slowly realized there was a disconnect between whom I said I was and my actions during the 2012 Presidential Campaign. Voter registrations were happening at *Shakespeare In The Park* and other surrounding places, places I now believe were safe for volunteers and may not have made an impact. One typical day in Harlem, people were roaming about, and I ventured out on my block. I wondered who was and was not registered to vote. Then, I realized that I should approach as many people as possible to inquire about their registration and overcome my fear and judgement when approaching them. I was mature enough to know at the moment I was uncovering a self-revelation. Although I was in my own neighborhood, I was working new territory for the sake of community service. I realized then exactly what Jesus meant when He said to the scribes "Love Thy Neighbor as Thyself."

I got clear on my inconsistencies. I did not have to "go" anywhere to do what I said I would do and be whom I say I would be. It was right on my block. Service was not some other place. I was not making love to my block, but that quickly changed. I began making love to the crowd. I began introducing myself to people and truly finding common ground with them. I realized that if I'm going to make requests of people, I should at least know them on first name bases. I realized that by calling the police or asking them to get off my stoop, I was doing what had always been done. I was treating people the way they had always been treated, especially by newcomers to the neighborhood. So after I began introducing myself to people on my stoop, my request for them to get off my stoop changed to "Can you make sure it's clean before you leave?"

And Then Some...

Through this experience I am clear that I was supposed to learn:

1. *To have courage and be the first to say hello.*

2. *To know that your interactions have purpose.*

3. *To let go of what you think others might think of you.*

4. *"Thou shalt love thy neighbour as thyself" - Matthew 22:39 KJV*

5. *Know that "Only what you have not given can be lacking in any situation" - A Course In Miracles Text-17.VII.4*

6. *"Withhold not good from them to whom it is due, when it is in the power of thine to do it" - Proverbs 3:27 KJV*

7. *Do what you have never done to get what you have never had.*

8. *Make people feel welcome.*

CHAPTER FIVE

KEEP A SERMON IN YOUR POCKET

Don't Just Manage; Inspire and Be Ready for It.

In 2010, a young man was receiving a scholarship during the National Urban League's Annual Legislative Policy Conference in Washington, DC. He was receiving the award in front of Senator Kirsten Gillibrand (D-NY), and when given the microphone to speak…he was at a loss for words. Everyone understood. He was an excited teenager. His life was changing. During the moments of the young man trying to figure out what to say, the National Urban League President and CEO Marc Morial supported him by grabbing the microphone and saying, "It's alright, we understand." He also announced to the crowd, "Always keep a sermon in your pocket."

It can be very easy to manage a program, project, task or situation. Leadership is about inspiring others to access their brilliance. Everything isn't a story, or a speech or a lecture, but the messages emerging from your leadership should inspire others. What's your sermon? Tap into your creativity, which will support you in crafting words and demonstrating actions that reveal new possibilities for the listener.

Before attending a meeting or an event, always have three points to discuss. (1) Begin with the inspiration. Think about why you and everyone else is present. You may even tell a story about yourself. Authenticity and vulnerability create openings in the soul of the listener. (2) Next, you should transition to the current state of your team, department or organization. (3) Lastly, close with what's next and what's possible for the listener or the organization. Additionally, state the impacts those occurrences will have.

And Then Some...

1. *Do your research and know your audience.*

2. *Begin with an ice-breaking story that sets the tone, causes the room to focus.*

3. *Make eye contact throughout the room as you speak.*

4. *Build people up with your message.*

5. *Include action items, asks or next steps.*

6. *Don't be afraid to wing it.*

7. *Keep it concise and brief.*

CHAPTER SIX
GIVE THEM WHAT THEY WANT

Your Brand

Look your best - who said love is blind?

~ Mae West

You are the celebrity the world has been waiting for. Picture it...you grace magazine covers and red carpets frequently. You are on stage for the performance of a lifetime. Everyone has come to see you and the show must go on! Think about it. If we buy a ticket to see Beyonce, we want to see her shake real hard and whip her hair. It's expected. We want Madame First Lady Michelle Obama to have amazing arms. We expect Oprah to do something amazing and alter lives with just an idea. We expect it. We expect Madonna to be outrageous and Janet Jackson to speak in a soft voice. We expect a politician to be charismatic and his wife to be the epitome of proper decorum. The world has the same expectation of you, to be your best!

It's important to own your visual brand. You should make sure who you are and what you are up to is represented visually. Many reject the notion that "what I wear matters," but the truth is, it does. First impressions are important.

And Then Some...

1. *Be proactive and avoid feelings of being underdressed or out of place. Confirm event attire and get examples of what it looks like.*

2. *Have a budget for purchases.*

3. *Polish your looks, make sure clothes are clean, neat and in good-repair.*

4. *Purchase essential pieces.*

5. *Accessorize tastefully.*

6. *Get alterations.*

7. *Get ideas from magazines and others. It's ok to be classic and add in trends.*

8. *Remember your visual brand extends to your social media.*

Switch Up the Game a Bit

"If you talk to a man in a language he understands, that goes to his head. If you talk to him in his language, that goes to his heart."

~ Nelson Mandela

Remember when some of us realized there was a difference from the way we spoke at home and the way other people talked, especially if those people were not of our same ethnic groups? When dealing with other people outside of your ethnic group, have you ever had to defend why or how you said something? Did you have a moment where you realized what you said matters and how you said it mattered even more? Did you have that aha moment while realizing you must speak one way at work or amongst colleagues and another way with your social network? I surely have, so much so I worked on my speech, pronunciation and choice of words. I looked up words in the dictionary I didn't understand and expanded my vocabulary. While in college, my community of black friends would correct each other's speech and support 'excellence.' We all subconsciously and consciously knew it was important to be able to speak the king's english while looking for a job, being at a job, and interacting in a majority world. We knew, and still know, to call it 'code switching,' or speaking one way with your peers and another way with the majority. It is a life skill that can take time to master. I've also been in situations where someone, a minority or someone of humble beginnings, didn't know how to code switch. Have you ever been in that situation and cringed every time they used improper subject-verb agreement or used slang? When giving the people what they want, not only is your visual brand important, your verbal brand is equally important. Learning how to "code switch" isn't betraying who you are. It is a means of increasing your effectiveness and tools. Once you learn how to code switch in one area, you begin to realize that you can communicate with anyone. You may even desire to learn another language.

And Then Some...

1. *Listen to others that talk differently from you.*

2. *Choose words you struggle with and break those words down into sounds.*

3. *Record yourself.*

4. *Practice with a partner or the mirror.*

5. *Know that it's ok to use words that are authentic for you. However, they just may require set up or follow up, such as "as they say in some circles."*

CHAPTER SEVEN
EVERYBODY WANTS A PIECE

Fill Your Own Cup

I was chapter president of the New York Urban League Young Professionals (NYULYP) and Northeast Human Resources Consultant for Archstone Apartments; however, I was depleted due to regional travel for work and countless meetings, day and night. I was emotionally conflicted. I knew God blessed me with both opportunities, yet I didn't understand why it was so taxing. Whether it was conflict on the chapter board, competition and challenges at work, or the fear that one or both worlds would completely unravel, I began to realize I had very few people in my circle who understood my situation or even cared. Dara Kalima, a chapter member of NYULYP, once quoted her father saying, "If you want something done, give it to the busiest person," and that was exactly how I felt. As I was learning how to lead volunteers, I realized people brought their issues and challenges to me to solve instead of me empowering or coaching them to solve their problems for themselves. Other times, I just felt used. I got plenty of calls to get tickets to an event or access to someone or something, but rarely did I receive a call from someone asking, "How are you?" or "How can I support you?" As I researched habits and practices of very successful people, I realized that I had to fill my own cup. I realized I needed to do 'self-filling' activities to keep my sanity and well-being and to perform at the level that was required of me.

I initially gathered biblical scriptures, quotes and affirmations that supported my God-given, universal, supernatural ability. I read those collected writings throughout the day and before and after major events. I found peace and solace knowing my leadership was ordained according to the many dogmas. I went further into health and wellness activities such as yoga, meditation and making better food choices. Basically, I nourished my mind and body.

I now realize how much work it was for me to stay emotionally balanced. I admit I often felt like I was on the verge of falling apart but I kept it all together. I now know my 'come from' was a scarcity mindset. At that time, my scarcity mindset operated as if 'there wasn't enough." As hard as I worked to balance it all, it was work to do that. After years of giving everything I had, years of feeling spent and years of feeling I was used for my work, I finally admitted to my coaches and fellow participants in my leadership team with Momentum Education that "the more I gave, the more people took from me." The feedback from my coach was I was operating from a place of scarcity.

Scarcity

The scarcity mindset is the view of life that supposes "the cup is always half empty." People with the scarcity mindset view the world through the vantage point of "I" rather than "we" or "us." This viewpoint extends to money and recognition. Rarely are they happy for others. They tend to be conspiracy theorists who believe someone is running a scam or maneuvering the upper hand to get ahead. They experience a never-ending hustle, fatigue, broken relationships, and constant struggles. The irony is they never voice these issues to anyone and would deny they even experience them, even if someone asked or figured out they do. That was the way I was. I had no clue I was operating that way, but the results in my life yelled, "Scarcity!"

Abundance

The abundance mindset is the view of life that supposes "the cup is always half full." People with the abundance mindset believe there is always enough, a solution and an outcome that involves everyone winning. These people have a deep sense of self-worth and security. They are in a constant state of creation because they know they matter and that all things are possible.

The real conversation I was having was that "I wasn't enough" and nothing I did would satisfy that. Everything I was doing professionally and some things in life felt like "I have to." As long as "I have to," there was no peace. The coaching supported me in seeing that I really didn't "have to" if I didn't want to and I could stop at any time. Sounds easy reading it, but at the time, I was too caught up in my image, and what I thought was expected of me and the list goes on. When I began to shift from scarcity to abundance, I began to access gratitude. I was grateful for having an amazing job, and I was grateful for support in my life. Tapping into the abundance began the shift. Even on the days when things didn't look so hot, I began to know that I am enough no matter what the outcome was. Now, I frequently check in mentally with my decisions and ask myself, "Am I operating from a scarcity mindset or abundance mindset?" Have you asked yourself the same question?

Scarcity	Abundance
Not Enough	More Than Enough
Takes Credit	Gives Credit

Sense of Entitlement	Sense of Gratitude
Talks About People	Talks About Ideas
Fears Change	Embraces Change
Hoards	Shares
Blames Others	Accepts Responsibility
No Goals	Goals
Breaks Word	Keeps Word
Chooses from Fear	Chooses from Love

And Then Some...

1. *Use affirmations, scriptures or music to recharge.*

2. *Don't isolate yourself.*

3. *Share what is on your heart with others.*

4. *Ask for feedback.*

5. *Connect with your support structure often.*

6. *Take time to form your own opinion or someone may feed you theirs. Where I'm from they say, "A dog brings a bone, a dog carries a bone..."*

THE LAW OF YES LEADERSHIP

As time went on at my first job after college as a human resources professional, I grew, but I didn't thrive. I realize now, I was over-committing myself in many ways. I also grew with the volunteer organization which I enjoyed. I appreciated being involved in the community. I appreciated being involved in the conversations concerning what was next. I spent four years as a Recruiter, then as an Employment Manager with a locally owned and operated company. Subsequently, I transitioned to an international corporation with a union environment where I stepped up my game. That's when I began to thrive. I often think about my very nurturing boss who put me in the forefront. He was my first champion, sponsor and advocate. He was committed to contributing to my learning, even at times when I wasn't. One of the first lessons he taught me was, "Raise your hand to projects and committees." In a nutshell, be a "yes." He was also a "yes" in my life because of our relationship, mentoring sessions and advocacy. As my career grew and my network expanded, I had the privilege to witness "yes leadership" in others. I believe when you say yes, the universe will provide support, abilities, opportunities, and learning experiences.

CHAPTER EIGHT

YOU CAN RUN BUT YOU CAN'T HIDE

"Disobedience is Witchcraft"

~ My Mother

Ever heard the phrase, "God is dealing with me"? I now realize that saying is the acknowledgment and awareness of a supernatural and universal lesson taking place in someone's life. My lesson was surrender.

What you run from will eventually find you. I ran from New Orleans because I sensed a spiritual calling only later to step into that calling in New York City. In actuality, I have always known that I would minister or "preach" as I call it. I've always known this deep down inside my soul. That level of knowing felt spooky to me. As a teenager in New Orleans, I had an uncanny sense that my spirituality would not be for a church or exist behind a pulpit. I knew that it would be bigger than I knew 'religion' to be, but I didn't know exactly what that was or how it would manifest. This "knowing" was very odd to me, and I dabbled in what I thought of as counter-culture activities such as poetry, going to reggae clubs, and so forth in an attempt to find "it." I was scared, and I sometimes wondered, in my teenage and young adult New Orleanian mind, if that was what voodoo felt like. Whatever I felt was always present, and again "I knew." I also knew that whatever it was, I would somehow surrender to it. The thought of surrendering was frightening to me!

Sometimes, it would whisper to me. It would nudge, yearn, draw me in. It felt like a constant "accept" or "seek." It would pull at me so strongly that I knew I would give in. I wanted to see what was on the other side of it. In 2013, during a tumultuous year of my life, a silent voice inside my head said, "I have something else for you." It was during the time that I was campaigning for the national leadership role with the Urban League Young Professionals. I heard it over and over again, and it did not startle me. Yet, it was in contrast to my immediate goal at hand, winning. That being said, I lost the election, but I was at peace because the inner voice/inner knowing stayed with me the entire time..."I have something else for you." I was willing to give up what I had to have what I did not have. I came to realize that what I didn't have, revealed itself by my loss. Beyond a shadow of a doubt, I knew it was meant to be. I surrendered to the spiritual voice that had been with me since I was a young adult. I became an ordained minister, calling myself, not just a minister, but a leadership minister. We all have a ministry, our unique ability is our ministry, and it's given to us to share. Leadership and self-development are important to me. I remained authentic to that. I reignited my consulting business, and I began to share with others that I was a student of "A Course in Miracles." Surrendering to the calling allowed me to embrace my gift of connecting with others. As a result of stepping into the calling, many things that I knew intellectually, dropped down to my heart, and I experienced myself as a leader, friend, and confidant. Let me tell you, the feeling is priceless! Surrender gave me permission to bring joy to others. Before, I was trying to "control" that feeling. Now, I listen to it and let it speak through me. My impact has deepened because of my surrender. My head and heart combined, and I realized I did not need a title or permission to do what I was called to do...all I had to do was be, and I would have.

In another situation a couple of years later, I was counseling a supervisor who had come to me for guidance. He had been placed on final warning because of a verbal altercation with another supervisor. He was at his wits end. After listening to his side of the story, I realized my job was to support him to look in the mirror. I shared with him, that whatever triggered him about the other person was what he was unwilling to deal with in himself. His eyes watered. He admitted to me that at times he felt others were trying to take advantage of him. Thus, if any of his direct reports slacked from doing work, he equated that to them trying to take advantage of him. Yet, he did not consider that his point of view applied to himself. He never gets to slack off he thought. If he was being taken advantage of by others, he actually was unwilling to admit that he had taken advantage of others as well. My response to him was, "I know what you mean...I've surrendered to the fact that I'm called to be a leader at all times when others get to goof off. There is no way around it, and no way for me to avoid it. I have accepted the fact that when assembled with others, I rise to the occasion. I am a leader!"

One night, while volunteering with transformation training, I had a splitting headache. It was odd because I normally don't get headaches. This one was serious; so serious that I chose to sit out several rounds of volunteering. I decided I was going to rest until the person I sponsored was up next. During my second attempt to sit out of the activity, the trainer came to the waiting area and said, "We have people in here who need support!" In a nanosecond, I went from wanting to respond to moving into action. While supporting others during the activity, I kept shifting my mood from being a victim to being someone who was in action and in contribution.

"My head is killing me!" I thought. "He doesn't know how I feel. I'm always here to support." Then I thought, "Why do people hold me to a higher standard than others?" I paused. In that moment I got clear that my thoughts about being a victim were making the entire night about me instead of making it about being in contribution to others. Secondly I realized, "Yes, I'm always held to a higher standard than others because I am a leader. Although I judge or interpret others as slacking off or taking the easy route as not contributing as much or being in excellence; it has absolutely nothing to do with who I am called to be and how I show up on the planet." Because I'm a leader, I get to "put in what's missing." After that realization, I also realized my head was hurting badly, and in that state, I was no good to "nobody." I responsibly decided to leave for the night. No story, no upset. On the next day, I gained a new awareness, and I texted the trainers and staff members in acknowledgement of my breakdown in commitment, but not without recommitting to being in contribution at a later time.

And Then Some...

1. *Pay Attention. Watch for the patterns and see the signs. God, The Universe, The Source is always communicating with us. Sometimes we're not seeing the patterns and other times we hear what's being communicated to us, but we don't like what we hear.*

2. *Be Courageous. Some say "take one for the team." It takes courage to interrupt patterns, accomplish the impossible and do what's never been done before in your life, your family's lives or anyone you know. If it's on your heart, it's for a reason so you must take the risk. You will never know the man or woman you can become until you do it and the universal lesson will keep appearing until you risk in a way you never have before.*

3. *Chill. Learn how to meditate and or pray. Quiet time opens up your heart and makes way for "The Voice."*

4. *Your gift is not just for you. It's coming through you for the planet. Get busy.*

5. *Delayed obedience is disobedience.*

Tell the truth to yourself about yourself

American novelist, essayist, social critic and author of two books I love, "Go Tell It On the Mountain" and "Giovanni's Room," James Baldwin is quoted saying, "Not everything that is faced can be changed, but nothing can be changed until it is faced."

This quote awakens the question in me, "What are you unwilling to face?" With many global social injustices and too many political inequities to count, I've come to realize the hardest battle we will ever face is the internal struggle with ourselves. What are you unwilling to face?

In 2005, Hurricane Katrina blew me to New York with two pairs of jeans and three shirts. Bewildered and ashamed, I didn't want anyone to know. I went on with each day and just wanted to be a new New Yorker, have no New Orleans accent and move on with the rest of my life. I was unwilling to face what happened.

Over the years, if anyone connected me to New Orleans and ultimately asked or inquired about anything "Hurricane Katrina," I would quickly change the subject. I was unwilling to face what happened to my loved ones and myself. It wasn't until 2012, while sitting at a brunch in Harlem, someone at the table learned I was from New Orleans and asked the question I dreaded the most "was your family affected by Katrina?" This was the ultimate question. This was the question which led me to change the 504 area code cell number I had since 1999. This question made me emotionally revisit the scene of what felt like a crime or tragedy each time. This was the question that seemed like the listener wanted to really ask, "How bad was it?" Well, the host of the brunch quickly answered, "That's the reason he came to New York." I became horrified and numb. All I could think was, "I don't want anyone to know because I can't handle talking about it."

Later that evening, I reflected. The host of the brunch was someone I called my brother, and the truth I knew in my heart was he would never do anything to hurt me. I had to be honest with myself... it was the truth. I arrived to NYC because of Hurricane Katrina. I was not recruited by a Big Four firm. I had not attended a school in the area, nor did I ever think, "This could be me." In that moment, I accepted that the circumstances of my arrival to NYC were in fact the truth. I began to face what I was unwilling to deal with.

I began to look at what I avoided. I avoided talking about how much Katrina broke my heart. I avoided talking about the shame of being called a "refugee" in America, as an American. I avoided talking about how my grandmother passed away shortly after Katrina. I avoided being embarrassed to say a devout Catholic woman had to wait to be buried because New Orleans barely had morticians to do the funeral services. I avoided talking about the post traumatic stress of wondering when the next moment or lifestyle would be taken away from me. The healing began the moment I faced the hurt, the anger, the shame and the heartbreak.

The best way to support our communities is to do the work within ourselves. Healing is on the other side of what we are unwilling to deal with.

And Then Some...

1. *Only God's Plan for Salvation Will Work - A Course In Miracles Workbook Lesson 71. Let go of grievances against, people, places or things.*

2. *Surrender is an upward action. It's about connecting with our source of origin to maximize our effectiveness and impact.*

3. *"Verily, verily, I say unto you, He that believeth on me, the works that I do shall he do also; and greater works than these shall he do unto my Father." John 14:12 KJV*

What works did Jesus do?

1. Heal the sick

2. Raise the dead

3. Change hearts

4. Inspire others

If He raised the dead, WHAT ARE YOU WAITING ON? **You don't need permission to BE who you are called to BE.** Don't wait! Ask for forgiveness, not permission. Don't wait! You have the authority to have your dreams come true. You have the power to heal your family. You have the wisdom to BE the leader you desire to BE. Most importantly, you have the ability to love.

CHAPTER NINE
ON KENDALL

During one of my monthly Urban League regional conference calls with a team I was elected to serve for two years, I snapped. A leader who wanted to be warm, but firm, finally snapped. Month after month, weekly update after weekly update, and call after call, no matter how hard I tried, no matter how connected, available and responsible I tried to be, I could not get chapter presidents to come to the call prepared with their monthly numbers. These were numbers of affiliate (branch office) and overall volunteer service hours, as well as any monies given to the affiliate that the Young Professionals chapters measured their success of providing services and dollars. Many Young Professionals chapter presidents had advanced degrees, high profile and highly responsible positions with their employers and in their communities, yet they could not come to a call for which they had 30 days to prepare and collect the information they should have been intimate with. So... I snapped.

Being Mr. Nice Regional Vice President got me nowhere. I had to ask, "Is it me, or is it you, because I am at a loss." Three voices on the call said, "It's not you, it's us." One of the voices was the young president of a fledgling chapter. She was new to this world of seasoned volunteers, and she was doing everything in her power to build her team and lead them. Her name was Kendall. She was willing to learn, and her team was venturing into new territory. Her #1 issue was people on her team being resistant to everything while offering no solutions. I realized that she took ownership for not being prepared. I called her immediately after the call with all the presidents. I let her know that that my snapping on the call was more so directed at the seasoned leaders. I also let her know I knew she was working hard. Kendall then replied "No Rahshib, I wasn't ready, and I want to be sharp." I hung up the phone with such great pride thinking, "That's what I'm talkin' about! She's got it" I had crazy respect for her in that moment.

Every so often, you see a young adult stand in a desire for excellence and build, lead, strive and accomplish. I was witnessing greatness in Kendall. Later I realized she was simply saying 'yes' to possibilities within herself, yes to her team, yes to the people in her chapter and community, and yes to the Urban League Young Professionals affiliate. When so many people get 'no's' day in and day out she was a YES all the time. She reminded me to be a yes to myself and my commitments.

And Then Some...

Yes Leadership is:

1. *Courage to face challenges, ask for support or stretch beyond your usual "good enough."*

2. *Commitment to keep integrity with your word, finish what you start and do it in excellence.*

3. *Willingness to take coaching. If someone cares enough about you to give you feedback...listen.*

CHAPTER TEN

THERE'S ALWAYS A BIGGER FISH

*If you were raised in a black church, you know all too well when
"mother" (an elder) gets the microphone, she will not turn it over
until she has thoroughly testified about how long she's been on the bat-
tlefield, and how good God has been to her. There is no way around
it...that moment after a long service when you're hungry, tired and
ready to watch football, then "mother" gets the mic. We must be at
peace with the process, and we're going to sit there until she finishes!*

Manage Up

Over the years, I've had big jobs and was always in charge of
heartbeats. As a human resources professional, my lane or set of
duties and level of responsibility includes anything that has to do
with managing and developing people. I do not manage dollar signs
or the front of the house, but I work with people who do. I let them
do what they do best. Essentially, I seat myself at the table with the
leadership of any company and offer solutions, inject, stop, redirect
and focus any conversation that involves the management of others
(heartbeats)...because it's my lane. Often times we let someone else
make decisions concerning something that's in our lane! Narrow the
focus and don't give your power away. When you narrow your focus
and stay in your lane, you create results that speak to your unique
ability. Don't get me wrong, knowing the drivers of your business
is key. Learn all you can about the other aspects of your business,

because you will be able to weigh in on a subject from the vantage point of your lane.

Once upon a time, what had happened was, there was a woman named "Lena Kilgore." She was the national chief learning officer of a startup company. Throughout her career, she was powerful enough to manage any conversation, product or concept that involved training, standards or best practices. Basically, she operated in her lane...the fast lane to be exact. At the time she was recruited to the startup, the company was paying $25K a month to a consultant who was flown in from another state every week.

I know...where do I sign up? The consultant was tasked with identifying best practices, creating customer service training and documenting standard operating procedures. In true stereotypical consultant fashion, he attempted to have everyone else in the startup do the work. Basically, the consultant talked a good game, but never produced tangible results. I know...why didn't anyone figure this out and save costs on his fee? When the chief learning officer got wind of what he was or was not doing, something that dealt in her lane, she clarified the consultant's contract and reigned-in the random requests to others. Because Lena was powerful in her authority and clear in her vision for the company's learning and development, the other executives supported her reigning-in the consultant. I can't say the consultant immediately began producing the results he was contracted to do, but everyone involved became clear regarding where the problem lay.

And Then Some...

1. *Know your unique ability.*

2. *Stay in your lane but understand other lanes to offer support from your unique perspective.*

3. *Manage up and be at peace with it:*

- *Gain a deeper understanding of your superior's management style.*

- *Time your communications.*

- *Problem solve versus puzzle piece.*

- *Align yourself with your superior's priorities.*

- *Extend yourself to make your superior shine.*

- *Adopt a team player attitude.*

CHAPTER ELEVEN
GET YOU SOME!

The streets often say "get your weight up" which basically means "step up your game" and increase your skills. The best getting for the Urban Professional is all things practical and theoretical. You've got to study something. Get theoretical in those books! You've also got to become practical. Do it! Practice it, and get it in your body, then repeat it.

If you, as an Urban Professional, are currently working in a position while aspiring to have that next-level position, then you should take the job description of that desired position and perform an honest assessment. Ask yourself, "What can I do and do well regarding this next-level position? Which areas do I not have experience in or what tasks have I not performed?" You' must be honest with yourself. Don't sugarcoat anything at all. This honest self-assessment will open doors for your next-level achievement. Once you have assessed that job description, hatch a plan! Map out when and how you will "get you some!" This is where the work will reveal itself to you. It's one thing to hatch a plan, but it's another thing to execute that plan. Execution of your plan will require commitment, passion, sleepless nights and countless moments of fantasizing about your vision to get it done!

While executing your plan, seek out thought leaders, not necessarily mentors, because this implies a commitment. Then, derive survey questions to directly ask those thought leaders. Next, schedule interviews, have meetings, go out for drinks with them, and get to the point! Here's some language to support you: "I'm currently working on my professional development, and I wanted to ask you a few questions about what makes you successful."

Try it, and see what happens. Many of us have years of experience outside the classroom and outside the realm of certifications and credits, and there is value in both practical and theoretical knowledge. Do not discount the classroom or study program because it may put context to content and validate what you always knew. It may also open you up to a new network of peers.

As a human resources professional, it was important for my career development to obtain my certification as a Professional in Human Resources (PHR). When searching for new job opportunities, it was not only the criteria companies looked for, but it also distinguished me from other candidates. You are "you" for a reason. We were created equal with individual assignments...some call that purpose. Our purpose distinguishes us from one another. Professional skills may be pathways for you to unleash, stand in and share your purpose with the world. As you get your skills game up, remember when you get, give back!

And Then Some...

1. *Do an assessment of your current knowledge, skills and abilities versus what is required of the position, path or purpose you are seeking.*

2. *Hatch a plan and find support who increase in areas you deem necessary.*

3. *Pay attention to the lessons along the way.*

THE LAW OF FEW

The Law of Few is often described as the 80/20 rule. 80% of the results come from 20% of all stuff. I've come to know this, and I have experienced that 20% is ok. Few is actually abundance. At any given moment, in any given circumstance...you have what you need!

Sometimes you have to encourage yourself.

1 Samuel 30:6...

My mother always said, "Do it for yourself, you'll feel better about it in the end!" That was her way of saying, "Don't wait on anyone."

When I was waiting on permission from someone else and waiting on support to show up, I realized that I was the best person to start with. If I simply began, then the resources would present themselves along the way on my journey.

CHAPTER TWELVE
YOU HAVE WHAT YOU NEED

WHERE I WAS. It was the fall season of 2011, and I was preparing my organization for the annual fundraiser in the Spring of 2012.

The event raised funds for high school students entering college. Up until then, it had been a few years since the annual fundraiser was successful. In 2007, it netted $11K. In 2008, it netted $145.00. In 2009, it netted $190.00. Yes, you read those dollar amounts correctly. I had become chapter president in 2009, and for the 2010 fundraiser, we netted $1K. However, this was not enough to change the lives of high school students in need. Assisting students at their "transition point" was important to the New York Urban League, and it was my desire to communicate the intention and need to others while inspiring them to participate.

Committee meetings began in Fall 2011, and there was excitement. The first meeting had thirty attendees, and so did the second meeting. We had the momentum and engagement we hadn't seen in years. Then something odd began to happen. Chapter members who were "volunteers"—like we all were— began to request payment as "consultants" to do what they joined the organization to do. Needless to say, I asked them to remove themselves from the planning, and the attendance at the meetings began to dwindle. When the number of attendees reduced to six of us, I began to panic. I began to question my ability to lead, the outcome of the event, the promise to high school students in need, and my legacy to the chapter. In the midst of my confusion, I trembled at my desk one day and asked myself, "What am I going to do? What am I going to do?" In that moment, a voice spoke to me saying, "You have what you need!" I immediately stopped trembling and thought, "What was that?"

Instantly the story of Gideon and the Midianites (Judges 7 KJV) came to mind—a story I haven't thought about since Sunday School. God allowed Gideon to be victorious over 120,000 men with only 300 men! You have what you need! I knew in that moment I had exactly the right-sized team to be successful.

THE OUTCOME OF THE EVENT? Not only did the event sell out, we netted $16K and donated $20K to the New York Urban League's Whitney M. Young Scholarships. A group of six people changed the lives of several high school students that year and forever.

And Then Some...

1. *I'm not focusing on the size, but the fact that it is singular. "...faith as a grain of mustard seed..." Matthew 17:20 KJV*

2. *Two fish and five loaves were few, but fed multitudes (Mark 6:37- 44 KJV).*

3. *Abundance is the simple fact that there is an unlimited source of everything we need or could ever want...infinitely available to all of us all the time. In that moment when you don't think you have enough...pause and say, "I have exactly what I need."*

CHAPTER THIRTEEN

MAKE ROOM

Prayer for the De-Clutterer

Are you willing to give up what you have to get what you don't have? Is what you are used to no longer serving you? What emotional, physical or psychological things are you holding on to, and what would happen if you released them? Many people believe we must de-clutter or clean up areas of our lives to embrace our higher selves. When you find yourself ready to release, this prayer may support you:

Lord,
In this moment I release anything that has held me back.
I know that You make all things new, and I trust in my renewal.
I trust in the possibility of making room for what You would have coming into my life.
I know the things I am releasing have served their purpose in my life.
Nothing is wasted, and I get to release and give as You have removed guilt, hurt, anger and resentment from my life, and given me love, forgiveness and joy.
Thank You.
In this moment, I call forward what serves me and my purpose.
I Am of service to the world. I Am a contribution. I Am Worthy.
I Am Enough and as my gratitude expands, so does my support.
Thank you. And so it is.

CHAPTER FOURTEEN
LAGNIAPPE

Leaders deserve ways to express themselves. In the years following my undergraduate studies, I often found myself exploring anything I didn't know anything about. I was hungry for spiritual and intellectual knowledge. I found myself at Cafe Flora and PoZazz Productions in New Orleans listening and learning. I was fascinated by the power in the spoken word. The following poems are what I created as a result of being in those spaces surrounded by that energy.

$42 Worth @ Erykah Badu Concert (House of Blues New Orleans)

Your eyes, Crimson Pillars-
Sunkissed Tips
Truth
Freedom
Earth
7
6
5
4
3
2
The one-ness of you and I
We are all connected
Do not deny

Truth
Freedom
God

Happy Days are here again

LOVE JUNKIE

They say it's a blessing,
They say it's a gift,
They say it's a miracle,
And I believe that it is.
Love conquers all,
Love changes everything.

I'm in a panic,
Like a fiend.
It's only you who can give me my fix.
Please, just one more time.
I've been waiting,
And I'll go the distance to get what I want.

When I'm near you,
It's like some mind blowing shit,
Stellar.
Oh yeah,
I can see 'em now,
Those diamonds in the sky.

When you open your mind
To my thoughts,
I release.
Take it, my fear
Take it, my insecurity
Take it, my shame
Take it, my guilt
Take it, my hurt,
And take my love
And do what you will.

I've been waiting so long,
For you to give me exactly
What I need.
You see, I escape in your arms,
And get lost in your warmth
And my soul gets lit
FIRE.
What would I do without you?
Fix me with your love.

©2001RahshibThomas

HE GOT GAME...on Jerome L.

Now,
I get the game that you got,
It's not
About me wanting you,
Rather you wanting life,
Excluding as much strife

As possible.

FREEDOM

Your ambition
Derives from from your past conditions,
But its does not hinder,
Your splendor,
Or candor.

You transcend pain
In your game.
Your game is so refined,
Premeditated,
Calculated,
And executed
With magnificent
Meticulous
Finesse.

AND I LIKE IT.

I'm inspired
By your desire.
You grew into a man
From a mustard seed.
Your countenance in the games says,
You got it,
And it ain't got you!
The ball is your only boo.

SWOOSH!

There's another one.

BOUT THAT LIFE : CONVO CONNECTION ACTIVITY

PURPOSE:

- *Tap into dormant thoughts.*

- *Connect with others about their thoughts and experiences.*

DIRECTIONS:

- *Answer each question.*

- *Once everyone is complete, go around the room soliciting answers per question.*

- *After each person has gone, open up the floor and solicit what emotions or thoughts came up for each person as they completed the activity or heard someone else.*

- *Point out any similarities.*

QUESTIONS:

1. *What is your favorite meal that is only served at certain times of the year?*

2. *What was your favorite game from your childhood?*

3. *What was your favorite candy from your childhood?*

4. *What is the first street address you can remember?*

5. *What is a favorite line from a song when you were 16 years of age?*

6. *Who is a hero in your family?*

7. *Who is a hero you admire from history?*

8. *Name a place you've visited that is connected to your heritage?*

9. *What phrase or statement from your childhood was used to scold you?*

10. *What phrase or statement from your childhood was used to motivate or inspire you?*

Have a Honey of a Day.

~ My Mother

ABOUT THE AUTHOR

Rahshib Thomas is a Speaker, an Author, and a Coach. Rahshib is the "Leadership Minister" of RT Consulting, where he supports his clients in the areas of motivational speaking, career coaching, strategy and branding. Rahshib's expertise derives from years of contribution as a Human Resources executive to high volume real estate and hospitality companies, specializing in labor relations, employee relations, performance management, and organizational development.

Throughout the years, he has partnered with the influential and impactful civil rights organization, the National Urban League, where he honed his acumen in community advocacy, non-profit management, volunteer management and fundraising. He was fortunate to hold local and national leadership positions as well.

Rahshib is an Ordained Minister and is studying and teaching 'A Course In Miracles,' a self-study system of spiritual psychotherapy. He also coaches in the area of transformational self-development, supporting learners experiencing love, impact and connection in all areas of their life.

Rahshib holds a degree in Mass Communications from the University of Louisiana at Monroe and certification as a Certified Professional (SHRM-CP) from the Society for Human Resources Management. Adding to his full life, he is an avid reader and enjoys television shows such as, Game of Thrones, most things on Netflix, anything Star Trek and of his favorite movies is "Paradise Road." He also enjoys a wide range of music and most importantly, he loves creole cuisine, especially his sister's gumbo!